OCEANS
IN 30 SECONDS

This library edition published in 2016 by The Ivy Press Limited,
an imprint of The Quarto Group
6 Orchard Road, Suite 100
Lake Forest, CA 92630, U.S.A.
Tel: +1 949 380 7510
Fax: +1 949 380 7575

Distributed in the United States and Canada by
Lerner Publisher Services
241 First Avenue North
Minneapolis, MN 55401, U.S.A.
www.lernerbooks.com

First Library Edition

A CIP record for this book is available from the Library of Congress.

ISBN: 978-1-78240-360-9

Printed in China

10 9 8 7 6 5 4 3 2 1

OCEANS
IN 30 SECONDS

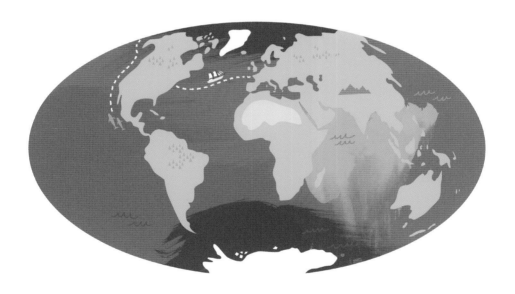

JEN GREEN

ILLUSTRATED BY WESLEY ROBINS

CONSULTANT: DR DIVA AMON

Contents

About this book
...in 60 seconds

Have you ever heard of the Blue Planet? Well, guess what... you are living on it right now! Over two-thirds of Earth's surface is covered by water and most of this is made up of salty seas and oceans. These underwater worlds are fascinating, deep, and dramatic. Get ready to dive in and explore.

This book will take you on a voyage of discovery, from the mighty forces that shape the shore and affect our weather to the deepest, darkest depths. For centuries the ocean remained a mystery and even now there is so much left to discover. Find out how tides are linked to the moon, visit coral kingdoms, and meet the weird and wacky creatures that live in the abyss. Uncover the perils of the seas, from shipwrecks to hurricanes, and read about the first ocean explorers.

The oceans play a vital role in our world today and we rely on them for food, travel, energy, and much more. But they are in danger. Learn how climate change and the actions of human beings are causing harm to our waters and find out about the things we can do to help save them.

Each ocean topic in this book has a page to read as fast as you like, to learn the main facts quickly. There's also a handy 3-second sum-up. Once you've read the basics, you can explore the watery world from the safety of dry land by completing the missions: create your own currents, make a volcanic island, and experiment with global warming. Now, strap on your life jacket and prepare to set sail.

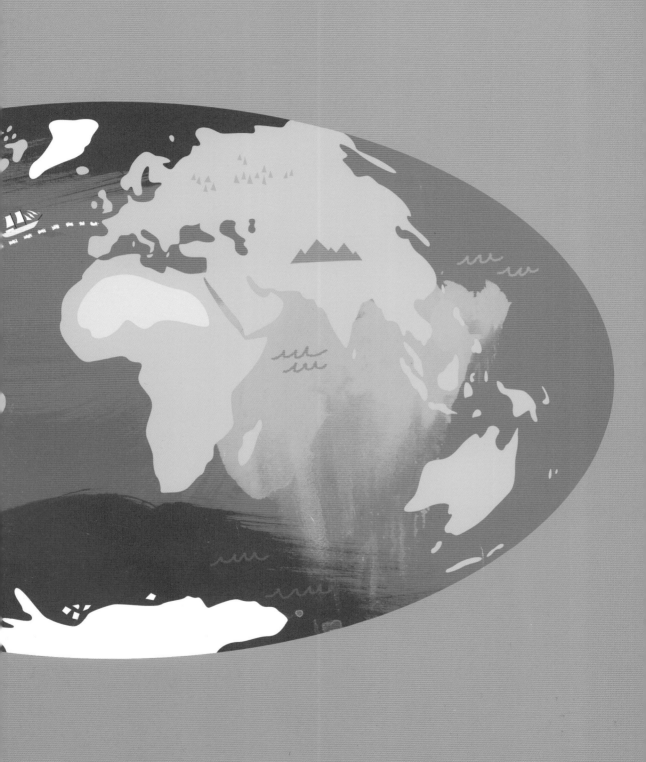

Blue planet

Planet Earth looks blue from space because water covers most of its surface. But only three percent of that water is fresh—the rest is saltwater seas and oceans. Natural forces such as the wind and waves keep the ocean water moving and shape our planet's surface and weather.

Blue planet
Glossary

buoyancy The force that allows something to float.

condense To change from a gas into a liquid.

crest The highest point of a wave.

current The movement of water in the sea or a river.

equator An imaginary line around the Earth, at an equal distance from the North Pole and the South Pole.

evaporate When liquid turns into gas.

gravity The force that attracts objects in space toward each other, and that pulls objects on Earth toward the center of the planet, so that things fall to the ground when they are dropped.

migration Movements of animals in large numbers from one place to another.

mineral A substance naturally present on Earth and not formed from animal or vegetable matter; for example, silver.

Northern Hemisphere The half of Earth north of the equator.

poles The two points at the opposite ends of the Earth, known as the North Pole and the South Pole.

Southern Hemisphere The half of Earth south of the equator.

Tropics The area just above and below the equator. The climate is warm or hot, and moist all year around.

trough The lowest point of a wave.

water vapor A mass of especially small drops of water in the air.

Oceans and seas

...in 30 seconds

When you go swimming at the beach, you are bathing in water that circulates through all of Earth's oceans and seas. This is because they are all connected, making one vast watery expanse.

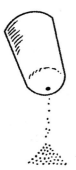

Earth has five great oceans: the Pacific, Atlantic, Indian, Southern, and Arctic oceans. There are also many smaller seas. Seas are usually waters near the coast, partly surrounded by land. Large, salty lakes inland are also called seas, but they are not part of the oceans.

The Pacific is by far the largest and deepest ocean. At its widest point, it stretches halfway around the world! At half the size of the Pacific, the Atlantic is the world's second biggest ocean. The warm Indian Ocean is partly fringed by coral reefs. The cold, stormy Southern Ocean surrounds Antarctica, while the Arctic is the smallest and shallowest ocean.

Oceans and seas are salty because the water contains minerals from the land, washed out to sea by rivers. Underwater eruptions and hydrothermal vents also release minerals. The main minerals, sodium and chlorine, make up salt.

3-second sum-up

Earth has five great oceans and many smaller seas.

3-minute mission Sink or swim?

Salt increases the density of water, making objects more buoyant. This is why it's easier to float in the ocean than in freshwater. You can test this at home.

You need: • Glass • Water • Egg • Salt • Tablespoon

1 Fill a glass with water.

2 Place an egg gently in the water. See what happens.

3 Remove the egg. Add two tablespoons of salt and stir briskly.

4 Put the egg in again. The salt gives added buoyancy, so the egg should now float.

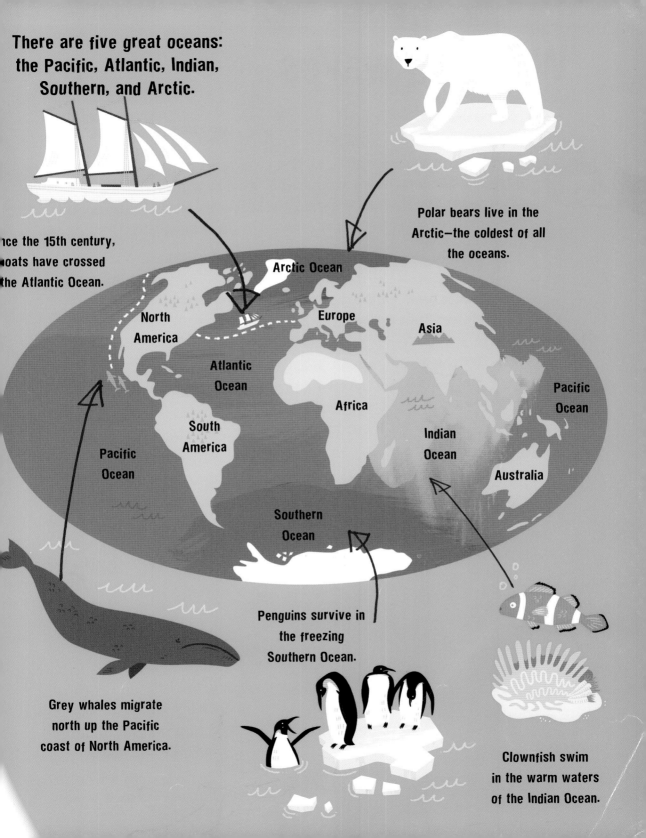

There are five great oceans: the Pacific, Atlantic, Indian, Southern, and Arctic.

Polar bears live in the Arctic—the coldest of all the oceans.

...nce the 15th century, ...oats have crossed the Atlantic Ocean.

Arctic Ocean

North America

Europe

Asia

Atlantic Ocean

Africa

South America

Indian Ocean

Pacific Ocean

Pacific Ocean

Australia

Southern Ocean

Penguins survive in the freezing Southern Ocean.

Grey whales migrate north up the Pacific coast of North America.

Clownfish swim in the warm waters of the Indian Ocean.

Wind and waves

...in 30 seconds

Ocean water is never still, as it is constantly moved by waves, tides, and currents. Waves are caused by wind blowing across the surface of the water. The stronger the wind, the bigger the waves it stirs up. The size and speed of waves are also affected by the water depth.

The highest point of a wave is called its crest and the lowest point in between crests is the trough. A wave's height is measured as the difference between the crest and the trough. Some waves are huge—gale-force winds can whip up waves of more than 49 ft (15 m) high.

Watching a stormy sea, you might think that the water in a wave moves far across the ocean. In fact, it moves in a circle and returns almost to the place where it started. That's why seabirds floating on the surface bob up and down in the same place.

Out in the deep waters of the open ocean, winds produce waves called rollers. When these waves move toward shallower water, the ocean floor blocks the circulation of water, so the waves rear up and break to form foaming crests. These breakers are the type of wave enjoyed by surfers!

3-second sum-up

Waves are made by winds blowing across the water.

3-minute mission Making waves

Try this experiment next time you take a bath. Alternatively, you could fill a plastic dish tub with water.

1 Blow gently across the water's surface. Even the faintest puff produces ripples.

2 Place a plastic duck or other floating object on the surface.

3 Blow again, but not directly at the object.

4 The object will ride the waves, but it should stay in about the same place.

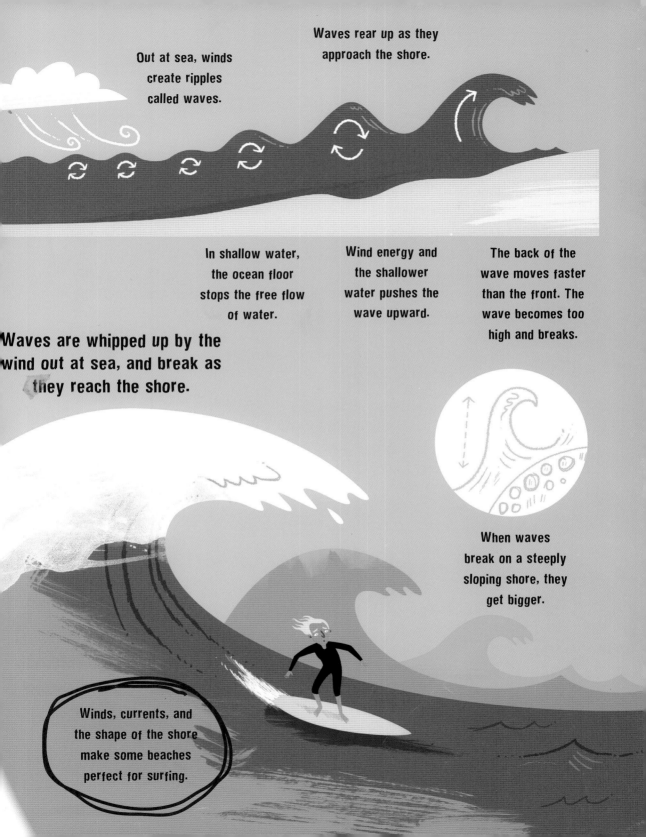

Out at sea, winds create ripples called waves.

Waves rear up as they approach the shore.

In shallow water, the ocean floor stops the free flow of water.

Wind energy and the shallower water pushes the wave upward.

The back of the wave moves faster than the front. The wave becomes too high and breaks.

Waves are whipped up by the wind out at sea, and break as they reach the shore.

When waves break on a steeply sloping shore, they get bigger.

Winds, currents, and the shape of the shore make some beaches perfect for surfing.

Tides

...in 30 seconds

Twice a day the sea level rises and water washes up the shore to flood beaches and harbors, then falls back again, leaving coasts high and dry. These changes are called tides.

Amazingly, Earth's daily tides are caused by the moon's gravity pulling on the oceans. As the moon circles our planet, its gravity draws large bodies of water toward it. This causes water to bulge in the area directly below the moon—causing a high tide. A similar mound forms on the opposite side of the planet. As Earth spins on its axis, the two mounds sweep across the oceans, bringing high tides to coasts across the world.

The sun's gravity also affects the oceans, but its pull is weaker. However, twice a month, the sun and moon line up, combining their gravitational pulls. This produces very high and very low tides called spring tides. At other times the sun and moon lie at right angles to one another, which cancels each other's pull, producing weak tides called neap tides.

3-second sum-up

Tides are mainly caused by the moon's gravity.

3-minute mission High and low water

Find out the distance between high and low tides on a trip to the beach.

1 On the beach, find the high-tide mark—a line of seaweed and debris that marks the upper limit of the tide.

2 At low tide, walk straight down to the water from the high-tide mark. Count how many paces you take.

3 Measure the distance you cover in one stride.

4 Multiply this measurement by the number of paces to find out the distance between the high- and low-water marks.

The gravitational pull of both the sun and moon creates the ocean tides.

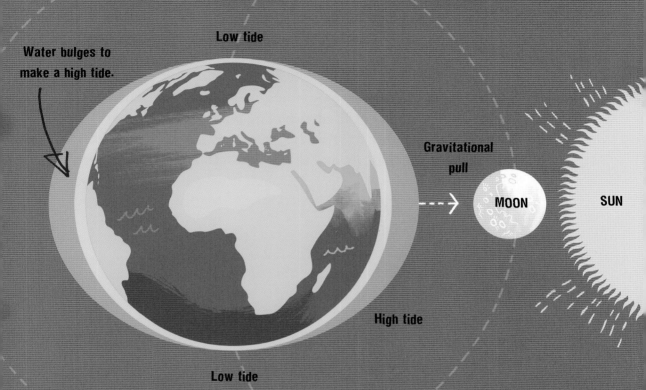

Low tide

Water bulges to make a high tide.

Gravitational pull

MOON

SUN

High tide

Low tide

Beach at low tide

Beach at high tide

Swirling currents

...in 30 seconds

Currents flow like rivers through the oceans. There are two main types of currents: surface currents and deepwater currents.

Surface currents are caused by winds blowing across the ocean's surface. Channelled by the surrounding land, these currents flow around in huge circles called gyres. They flow clockwise in the Northern Hemisphere and in the Southern Hemisphere they flow counterclockwise.

Surface currents help spread the sun's heat around the globe. Warm water from the Tropics flows north and south toward the poles. Cold polar currents flow toward the Equator, cooling nearby coasts. The cold Kamchatka Current, for example, flows from the Arctic to cool the warm waters surrounding Japan.

Deepwater currents are dense and cold. In some places, such as the polar regions, cold surface water sinks. In other areas, cold, deep water may rise, bringing mineral-rich water to the surface. These vertical currents are called downwellings and upwellings.

3-second sum-up

Surface and deepwater currents flow through the oceans.

3-minute mission Circling currents

You need: • Bowl • Water • Baby powder

1 Fill the bowl with water and sprinkle a little baby powder on the surface.

2 Blow gently across the middle of the bowl. The powder-covered water will flow in two circles, one turning clockwise and the other counterclockwise.

Your blowing breath is acting like the strong winds at the Equator that set ocean currents in motion.

here are two types
of ocean currents:
urface currents and
eepwater currents.

Sailboats need to take
notice of the wind and
of the surface currents.

This surface current
flows along the shore.

Upwellings bring cold
water rich in nutrients
to the surface.

Upwellings
rise from the
deep ocean.

Air and oceans
...in 30 seconds

There is a set amount of water on Earth, and it continually circles between the air, oceans, and land. As it moves, it changes from a liquid to a gas and then back again. This endless process of change is called the water cycle.

When the sun shines on seas, lakes, and rivers, heat causes moisture to rise into the air as water vapor. This process is called evaporation. The warm, moist air rises over high ground, where it cools, and the moisture condenses to form tiny water droplets or ice crystals, which gather to form clouds. When a cloud hits cooler air, the moisture inside it condenses again, then falls as rain. Rainwater drains away into streams and rivers, which empty into the oceans, and so the water comes full circle.

Oceans affect the weather in other ways as well. Places that lie in the path of moist winds blowing off the ocean experience a lot of rainfall, which is why coasts are generally wetter than areas far inland. Coasts also have a milder climate than inland areas because the ocean warms up more slowly than the land in summer and keeps its heat for longer. This keeps coasts cooler in summer but warmer in winter.

3-second sum-up

Moisture continually moves between the air, oceans, and land.

Prehistoric water?

Get a glass of water from the tap and put it next to you. Can you guess how old it is? The water may have recently fallen from the sky as rain but the water itself has been around as long as the Earth has. Earth has limited water so the water keeps going round and round in the water cycle. Maybe a dinosaur actually walked through a lake that contained the very water you are drinking!

Water circulates continually between the air, oceans, and land.

Solar energy

Clouds are made of water droplets or ice crystals.

Clouds form and rise as they move over land.

Water evaporates from the oceans' surface.

Snow melts and runs off mountains into streams.

Rain, hail, sleet, or snow falls from clouds.

Rivers return water to the oceans.

Stunning seascapes

The world's coastlines stretch for 722,223 miles (1,162,306 km)—that's more than 25 times the circumference of Earth itself. Coastline scenery, such as sheer cliffs and sandy beaches, is shaped by waves, tides, and currents. Other forces are at work, too, shaping the bed of the deep oceans and creating dramatic scenery, which can be seen both above and below the water surface and at the poles.

Stunning seascapes
Glossary

abyssal plain An underwater plain on the deep ocean floor.

continent One of the large land masses of Earth, such as Europe, Asia, or Africa.

continental island An island, close to a continent, that was once part of that continent.

continental shelf The underwater border of a continent that slopes gradually to the ocean bottom.

crust The outer layer of Earth.

current The movement of water in oceans or rivers.

erode To gradually destroy and remove the surface of something through the action of wind, water, or other natural elements.

glacier A large mass of ice, formed by snow on mountains, that moves, usually very slowly, down a valley.

groin Artifical construction that keeps sand in place on a beach.

headland An area of high land that sticks out from the coast into the ocean.

hotspot A weak point in Earth's crust where molten rock from deep underground forces its way onto the surface.

invertebrates Animals without backbones.

lava Hot, liquid rock that comes out of a volcano and hardens on Earth's surface.

longshore drift The movement of sand along the coastline caused by the wind and currents.

magma Hot, liquid rock found below Earth's surface.

oceanic island An island lying in the deep ocean, formed of erupting underwater volcanoes.

overriding plate The tectonic plate that overrides another plate when the two meet.

poles The two points at the opposite ends of Earth, known as the North Pole and the South Pole.

sandspit A stretch of beach, formed by deposits of sand and mud, that sticks out into the ocean.

subducting plate The tectonic plate that, when two plates collide, dives beneath the other plate.

tectonic plate One of the huge sheets of rock that forms Earth's surface.

Ocean floor
...in 30 seconds

If you were to dive to the depths of the ocean in a submarine, you would find scenery as dramatic and beautiful as any on land. Near the shore, the water is shallow, as Earth's landmasses are edged by wide, flat continental shelves. Suddenly the ocean floor drops away to a vast plain, which is dotted with soaring peaks, volcanoes, and long chains of mountains. There are also sheer cliffs and yawning trenches. Welcome to the amazing world of the deep ocean.

The craggy peaks, volcanoes, and deep trenches are all formed by movement of the huge, rigid plates that form the Earth's crust. These tectonic plates are part of the land and are found below the oceans. The plates ride like rafts on the hot, molten rock below. Driven by currents in the molten layer, they inch slowly across the globe, clashing together, scraping past one another or pulling apart.

Where two plates are pulled apart, molten rock surges up to fill the gap. This forms volcanoes and, eventually, long lines of mountains where the plates meet. Where two plates collide, one is forced to dive below the other, forming a deep trench. If two plates scrape past each other, the rubbing action can cause earthquakes.

3-second sum-up

The ocean floor has mountain chains, volcanoes, and deep trenches.

Make your own tectonic plates

Take a hard-boiled egg and crack its shell. The shell is Earth's outer crust, divided into plates. The egg is the outer surface of Earth. If you move the pieces of shell around, it breaks in some places and exposes the egg. The same thing happens on Earth, but on Earth, it creates mountains, earthquakes and new ocean floor.

Continental shelf

A seamount
is an underwater
mountain.

The ocean floor slopes
steeply to deep ocean.

An island forms
where an underwater
volcano breaks the
surface of the water.

Abyssal plain

An ocean trench forms
where plates collide.

A mid-ocean ridge is
a chain of underwater
mountains, dotted with
volcanoes.

Overriding plate

Subducting plate

When plates
collide one
dives below
the other.

The dramatic ocean floor
is formed by the
movement of Earth's
tectonic plates.

Shaping the shore
...in 30 seconds

Coasts are border zones where the land meets the ocean. In a process called erosion, wind and waves wage constant war against the solid rock edging the world's continents and islands.

Waves beat against the shore every minute of every day. This constant motion varies from gentle lapping in calm weather to violent storm waves crashing into the land. Waves fling sand, rocks, and pebbles against the shore. These act like sandpaper, scouring away, or eroding, the land.

The speed at which land is eroded depends on the rocks that form the coast. Soft rocks, such as chalk, erode quickly, forming curving bays and coves. Hard rocks, such as granite, wear away more slowly, leaving craggy headlands jutting out to sea. In the end, even the hardest rocks give way to the constant pounding of the water.

3-second sum-up

Seawater wears away the land in a process called erosion.

3-minute mission War of the waves

You need: • Modeling clay • Square plastic dish tub or high-sided cake pan • Sand • Water

1 Mold three slabs of modeling clay about 1.5 in (4 cm) high, 1 in (2.5 cm) wide and 2.5 in (6 cm) long.

2 Lay the slabs along one end of the pan with the long edges jutting into the middle like headlands.

3 Place sand in between the headland slabs of clay, to represent soft rocks at the coast.

4 Add water at the far end of the container to 1 in (2.5 cm) depth. Lift it to slosh the water back and forth. The soft "rocks" wear away quickly, like bays between headlands.

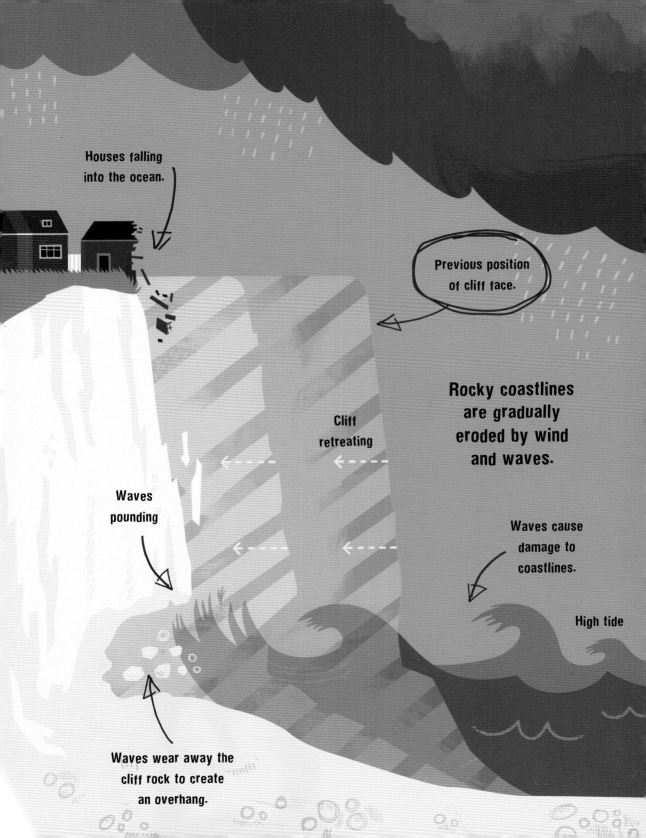

Rocks on the move

...in 30 seconds

Waves and currents don't always wear away the land. Along some coasts, they actually help to build it by moving material around the coast. Rocky debris, such as sand and pebbles, piles up on the ocean floor in coastal waters. Waves and currents sweep the debris along the shore. In the sheltered waters of bays and inlets, the current weakens and drops the debris. The debris washes ashore to form a beach. This process is called deposition.

Beaches can be rocky, pebbly, or sandy. Waves are at work here, too, smoothing pieces of rough-edged rocks into round pebbles. The stones are broken down over time, creating shingle beaches. Further erosion grinds the rock into fine pieces—sand. Billions of tiny, rocky grains fill a sandy coastline, with wind piling loose sand into dunes at the back of the beach.

A build-up of material can create new features. A sandspit is a pile of rocky debris that has formed a finger of land pointing out to sea in a bay or estuary. Sometimes, this line of debris reaches right across a bay to form a bar. The water behind it forms a salty lagoon.

Along some shores, sand or mud is dumped out to sea to form islands, which can shift along the coast during violent storms.

3-second sum-up

Waves and currents drop rocky debris to form beaches, sandspits, and islands.

Longshore drift

Where the waves strike the shore at an angle, they drag sand and pebbles along the shore. This process, called longshore drift, can sweep away whole beaches. Fences called groins are built at right angles to the beach to keep sand and pebbles in place.

Sand piled up by the wind forms a dune.

Waves and currents build shorelines by dropping rocky debris onto the land.

Beach

Dune

A sandspit is formed of sand or mud.

Longshore drift sweeps along the shore.

Groins keep sand in place.

Sand and pebbles are dropped by longshore drift.

Islands

...in 30 seconds

Islands are areas of dry land completely surrounded by water. There are two main types of island: oceanic and continental.

Oceanic islands lie a long way from land and are often the tips of underwater volcanoes. When a volcano erupts on the ocean floor, lava piles up to form an underwater peak called a seamount. If the eruptions continue, the seamount grows until eventually it breaks the surface and becomes an island.

An island chain forms in an ocean at a place called a hotspot. This is a weak point in the center of a tectonic plate where molten rock surges up through cracks to form an underwater volcano, which grows into an island. In time, the hotspot stays in one place, while the plate slowly slides over it. This means that when one volcano stops erupting, another one begins.

Continental islands rise from the shallow waters of continental shelves that edge the world's landmasses. When sea levels are low, they are part of the mainland. When sea levels rise, low-lying land becomes flooded, and hills become islands.

3-second sum-up

Islands are areas of land entirely surrounded by water.

3-minute mission Volcanic island

You need: • Small bowl • Water • Coins

1 Fill a small bowl with water to a depth of 1.5 in (4 cm).

2 Gently drop coins into the center of the bowl. Each coin represents a volcanic eruption.

3 As you add more coins, the "volcano" slowly rises and eventually breaks the surface to fo m an island.

Some oceanic islands are formed when underwater volcanoes erupt.

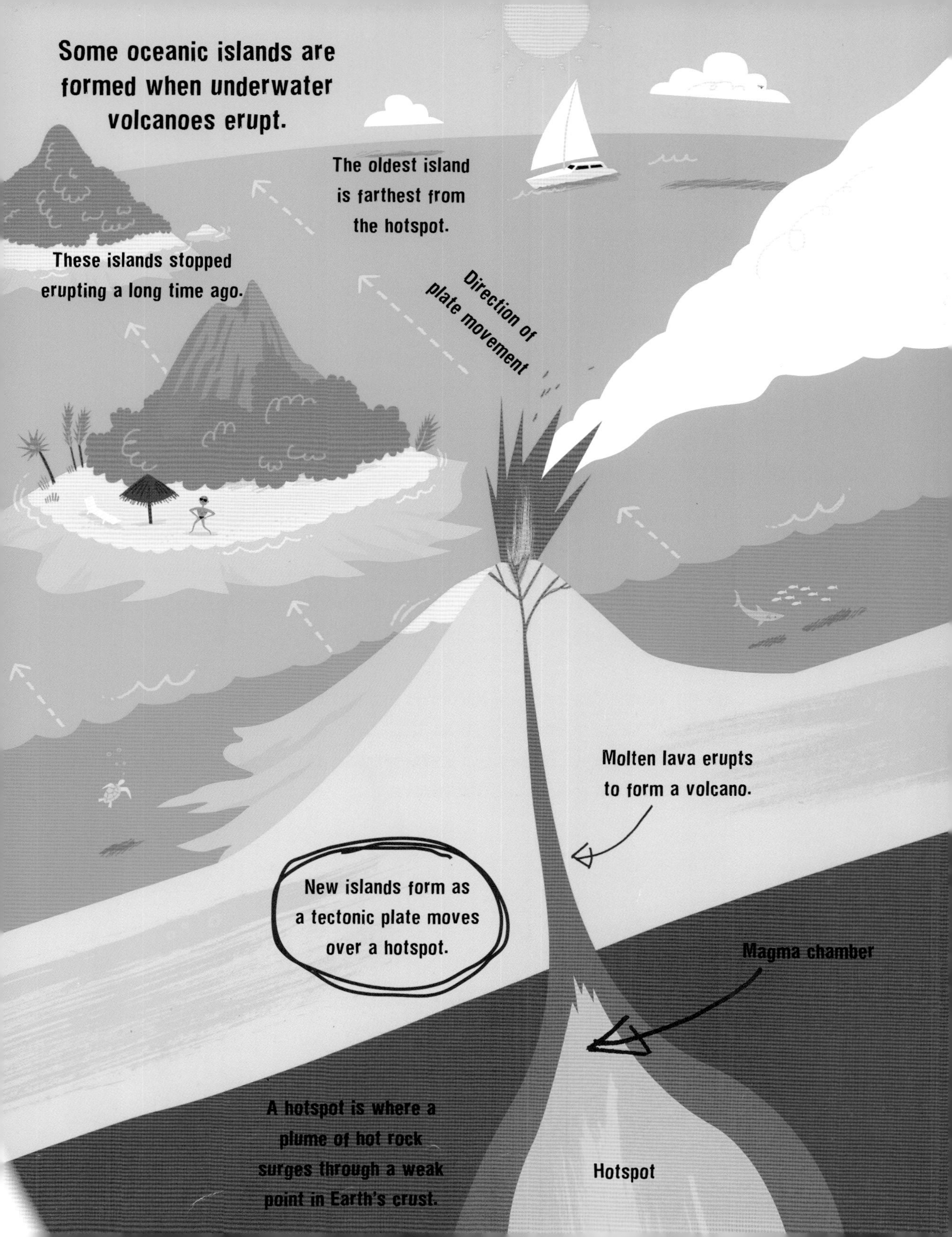

The oldest island is farthest from the hotspot.

These islands stopped erupting a long time ago.

Direction of plate movement

Molten lava erupts to form a volcano.

New islands form as a tectonic plate moves over a hotspot.

Magma chamber

A hotspot is where a plume of hot rock surges through a weak point in Earth's crust.

Hotspot

Polar seas

...in 30 seconds

Travel to the far north or south of our planet and you'll find the world's coldest and stormiest seas: the Arctic and Southern oceans. Polar seas look different from other oceans, as they are covered by floating ice for much of the year.

So why are polar seas so cold? The Earth's surface curves away from the sun at the poles, so the sun's rays are spread out over a wide area. This reduces their heating power. In winter, the sun never rises above the horizon, so it is dark for 24 hours a day, and bitterly cold.

Land in the polar regions is mostly covered by a thick layer of ice up to 2.5 miles (4 km) deep. Ice also flows down slowly from hills and mountains toward the coast, in the form of glaciers. When it reaches the coast, the ice spreads out on the ocean to form floating ice shelves. Huge chunks of ice from these may break off to form icebergs.

Carried by ocean currents, icebergs drift into warmer waters, where they can be a danger to ships. In 1912 the luxury liner *Titanic* famously struck an iceberg in the North Atlantic and sank. Only about one-tenth of an iceberg shows above the surface; the rest lies below.

3-second sum-up

Polar oceans are mostly covered by ice for much of the year.

Life on ice?

Icebergs may look lifeless, but that's not the case. Small plants called algae grow in between ice crystals or on the underside of an iceberg. Small fish hide from predators in ice holes and invertebrates feed on shrimp-like animals called krill. Seabirds can nest on icebergs as well.

Glaciers slowly flow down from high ground to the coast.

Dramatic features of polar coasts include glaciers, floating ice shelves, and icebergs.

An icebreaker ship can pass through ice.

A glacier on the coast forms a floating ice shelf.

A research station is home to scientists who explore the polar world.

Icebergs can be a menace to ships.

Ice sheets cover the land.

Ocean life

The world's seas and oceans are all linked to form one huge saltwater environment. In turn, this vast expanse can be divided into many smaller habitats, such as coral reefs, polar seas, and deep, dark trenches. Each habitat has different conditions that suit certain creatures.

Ocean life Glossary

Abyssal Zone The deepest ocean zone, 13,000—19,600 ft (4,000—6,000 m) below the surface.

carbon dioxide (CO$_2$) A gas breathed out by people and animals and also produced by burning carbon.

coral polyp One of the small creatures whose chalky skeletons build up to form coral reefs.

coral reef Structures in the ocean made from rock created by coral polyps.

food chain A system where small animals are eaten by larger animals, which, in turn, are food for even larger animals.

gills The parts of a fish that make it possible for it to breathe in oxygen.

habitat The natural environment of someone or something.

kelp A type of large seaweed.

microscopic Something that is so small it can only be seen using a microscope that magnifies it many times.

Midnight Zone A deep ocean zone 3,300—13,000 ft (1,000—4,000 m) below the surface.

migration Movements of animals in large numbers from one place to another.

oxygen A gas breathed in by people and animals, produced by plants.

pectoral fins Fins on a fish's chest that it uses for swimming and that flying fish use for flying.

phytoplankton Tiny plant life-forms in the ocean.

predator An animal that kills other animals for food.

prey An animal that is hunted and eaten by other animals.

submersible A small vehicle for underwater exploration.

Tropics The area just above and below the Equator. The climate is warm or hot, and moist all year round.

Twilight Zone A deep ocean zone 660—3,300 ft (200—1,000 m) below the surface.

zooplankton Tiny animal life-forms in the ocean.

Sunlit surface

...in 30 seconds

Each level of the ocean, from sunlit waters to the cold jet-black depths, is home to different animals. Sunlit waters are rich in oxygen, relatively warm, and full of life. This habitat has the greatest concentration of life in the oceans.

Plants of all sizes thrive near the surface, where they use sunlight to make food and to grow. Microscopic plants called phytoplankton drift in the sunlit zone, providing food for many animals. Forests of giant seaweed called kelp grow off rocky coasts in the Pacific. The waving fronds of giant kelp can measure 150 ft (45 m) in length! These underwater forests shelter fish, crabs, sea urchins, seals, and sea otters.

Animals that live in surface waters include jellyfish, which capture small prey, such as fish, in their stinging tentacles. Many surface-water fish have dark backs and pale bellies. This coloring, called countershading, helps them to hide from predators above (such as birds) and below (such as bigger fish). Fish have gills to filter oxygen from the water, but animals such as turtles must come to the surface to breathe air.

3-second sum-up

The sunlit surface waters of the oceans are full of life.

3-minute mission Swim like a fish

Fish, seals, and whales have smooth, streamlined bodies, shaped like torpedoes, that slip easily through the water.

You can test out how body shape changes movement in a swimming pool. Stand in the shallow end and try to walk normally. You'll find it's very difficult to do so because the water pushes against you, producing a force called drag. Now float on your stomach and swim forward. In this position your body is more streamlined, like the shape of a seal or dolphin. This reduces drag and makes it easier to move through the water.

Kelp forests are
one type of habitat
lit by sun.

The sun's rays
light up and heat
the surface waters.

Phytoplankton live
in the warm
surface water.

Dolphins breathe
air through their
blowholes.

Seabirds swoop down to catch
fish just below the surface.

Countershading
hides fish from
above and below.

Jellyfish use
stinging tentacles to
capture prey.

Sea otters dive
for sea urchins
to eat.

Some crabs sift
for food on the
ocean floor.

Kelp contains
air pockets to
help it float.

In the depths

...in 30 seconds

Only the upper layer of the ocean is sunlit and rich in oxygen. Below 660 ft (200 m) lies the Twilight Zone, which is lit only by faint glimmers from above. No light at all reaches the Midnight Zone below 3,300 ft (1,000 m). The inky-black, ice-cold waters below 13,000 ft (4,000 m), called the Abyssal Zone, are home to relatively few creatures. Many of these look weird and wonderful, but are perfectly adapted to the hostile world of the deep.

The deeper you go, the greater the weight of the water pressing down on you. The bodies of deep-sea creatures are built to stand up to this pressure, but they cannot survive without it. If brought up to the surface, they can explode!

Food is very scarce in the ocean depths, and no plants can grow in the darkness. Fish such as gulper eels have giant mouths and stretchy stomachs, so they can take advantage of any prey they come across. These fish can swallow prey two or even three times their own size!

The floor of the Abyssal Zone is mainly flat, and covered with a deep layer of sediment called ooze. Tripodfish live here, but these fish do not just swim. They have three long fins that act like stilts as they perch above the ocean floor, waiting for food.

3-second sum-up

Deep-sea animals survive cold, darkness, and great pressure.

Shine a light

Some fish in the deep ocean make their own light using special chemicals. Viperfish have a row of lights on their bellies to disguise their shadow. Flashlight fish switch their little lights on and off to attract a mate. Deep-sea angler fish have a long fin with a lighted tip dangling in front of their mouths. Fish that are attracted to the light are snapped up by its giant mouth.

eep-sea creatures
have adapted to
survive cold,
darkness and
pressure.

Flashlight fish have
pockets under their eyes
that give off light.

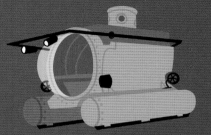

Submersibles can dive
to great depths.

The viperfish has huge fangs.

The deep-sea angler fish
hunts using a glowing,
built-in fishing rod.

The stretchy
stomach of the
gulper eel allows it
to eat prey much
bigger than itself.

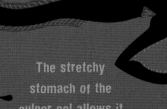

Some deep-sea creatures
give off light—this is called
bioluminescence.

The tripod fish has
pectoral fins that
direct food toward
its mouth.

Ooze—a sediment on the
floor of the Abyssal Zone.

Ocean food chains

...in 30 seconds

The oceans are a perilous place, where the rule is eat or be eaten. Sea creatures depend on one another for food. Diagrams called food chains show what these creatures eat.

Almost all ocean food chains start with plants. Unique among living things, plants use carbon dioxide (CO_2), dissolved minerals, and sunlight energy to make their own food and grow. This amazing process is called photosynthesis. Ocean plants include seaweed and sea grasses, but most plant life in the oceans is made up of microscopic plants known as phytoplankton.

These tiny plants are eaten by microscopic animals called zooplankton, which includes tiny shrimps and crabs. These minute creatures are eaten by small fish, which are in turn eaten by bigger fish. Powerful predators such as great white sharks and orcas (killer whales) form the top of the food chain. When animals die, their remains are eaten by scavengers such as shrimps and crabs. The minerals their bodies contain are recycled for plants to use. Nothing goes to waste.

3-second sum-up

Living things in the oceans depend on one another for food.

What's on the menu?

Did you know the largest creatures in the ocean feed on the smallest?

Great whales such as blue and humpback whales feed on plankton. So do the world's largest fish, whale sharks, and basking sharks. These giant animals open their mouths wide and gulp plankton-rich water. Fringed plates hanging down inside their jaws filter out the plankton, which is then swallowed.

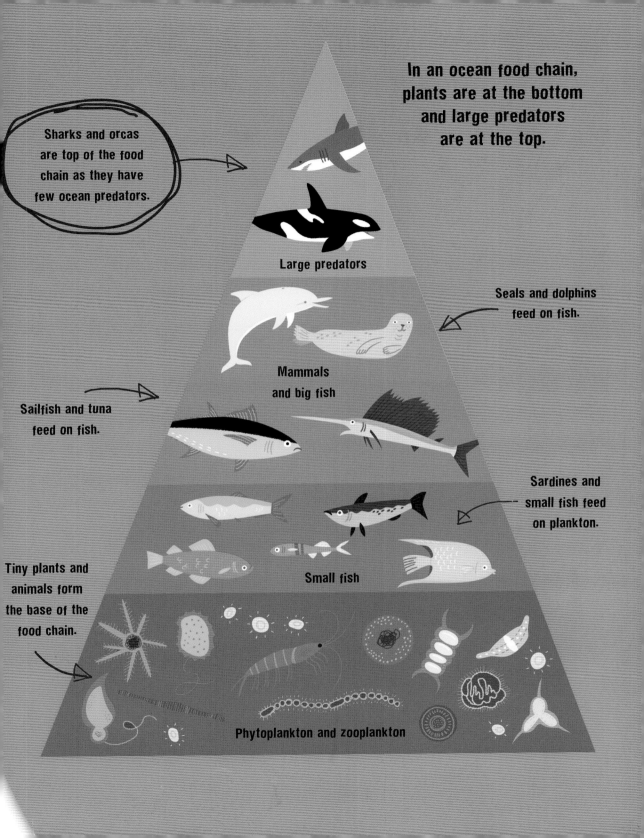

In an ocean food chain, plants are at the bottom and large predators are at the top.

Sharks and orcas are top of the food chain as they have few ocean predators.

Large predators

Seals and dolphins feed on fish.

Mammals and big fish

Sailfish and tuna feed on fish.

Sardines and small fish feed on plankton.

Small fish

Tiny plants and animals form the base of the food chain.

Phytoplankton and zooplankton

Coral kingdoms
...in 30 seconds

Coral reefs form in warm, shallow seas in the Tropics. The largest coral reefs are so huge they can be seen from space, yet they are built entirely by tiny animals called coral polyps.

Coral polyps are related to sea anemones. They have soft bodies protected by a chalky skeleton. When the polyps die, the skeletons remain and gradually pile up on top of one another to form a reef. This happens very slowly. A large reef such as Australia's Great Barrier Reef is thousands of years old.

Coral reefs are called the rainforests of the sea because, like rainforests, they teem with life. Reef creatures include brightly colored fish, octopuses, molluscs, and starfish. There are giant clams and large sea sponges. Each nook and cranny on the reef provides shelter for animals that are either active by day or come out to feed at night.

The Great Barrier Reef runs for 1,600 miles (2,600 km) off Australia. One of the reef's greatest enemies is a large, spiny starfish that turns itself inside out to feed on living coral. The crown-of-thorns starfish pushes its stomach out of its mouth and dissolves the coral with its digestive juices.

3-second sum-up

Coral reefs are built by tiny animals called polyps.

Slow growing

Coral reefs have existed for millions of years but less than 0.1 percent of the world's ocean floor is covered by them. They grow very, very slowly—anywhere from 0.1 to 4in (0.3 to 10 cm) per year—in warm, shallow, and moving water.

Icy habitats
...in 30 seconds

The Arctic and Antarctic are the coldest, harshest places on the planet. Very few creatures live on land there, yet polar seas are rich in wildlife. In spring and summer, plankton multiply on the surface, providing food for shrimps and krill, which in turn feed fish, whales, and other animals.

Birds and mammals that live near the poles keep warm with the help of a dense coat of feathers or fur. Seals, whales, polar bears, and penguins also have a thick layer of fatty blubber under their skin, which protects them from the ice-cold water.

Arctic mammals include walruses, the largest members of the seal family. Walruses are known for their long tusks, which they use to dig for shellfish on the ocean floor. Two small whales are found only in the Arctic. White whales or belugas are called "sea canaries" because of their chirping calls. Narwhals each have one long, spiraling tusk sticking out of their foreheads, like a unicorn's horn.

Antarctica is famous for penguins. Expert divers, they zoom through the water using their wings as flippers. The penguins' greatest enemies are leopard seals. These ferocious predators bump into the floating ice on which penguins are resting to tip them into the water.

3-second sum-up

Polar seas are rich in life, though few animals live on land.

Sea bears

Polar bears are top predators of Arctic waters and spend most of their life in the water or out on the sea ice. Their favorite prey is seals. They wait by the small holes in the ice that seals use for breathing. When a seal pops up for air, the bear kills it with one swipe of its enormous paw.

Many mammals are well adapted to live in the icy conditions around Arctic coasts.

Walruses use their tusks to pull themselves out of the water.

Polar bears feed on seals, killing them when they surface to breathe.

Belugas can easily swim underneath the ice as they don't have a dorsal fin.

Narwhals feed on fish, shrimp, and squid.

Belugas feed on fish, crabs, and shrimp.

Ocean journeys
...in 30 seconds

Not all animals spend their lives in one place in the oceans. Many use the seas as watery highways, traveling long distances to find food, escape the cold, or reach a safe place to breed. These long journeys are called migrations. Whales, seals, fish, seabirds, turtles, and lobsters all migrate.

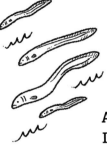

Imagine walking the length of a huge continent such as Africa and then, a few months later, turning around and trekking all the way back again. Many animal migrations are as epic as this. Blue whales swim from the Tropics to polar seas in spring to feast on plankton. In autumn, they swim all the way back to breed.

Arctic terns breed in the Arctic in summer when it is light 24 hours a day. In autumn they fly south all the way to Antarctica where summer is just beginning. That's 9,300 miles (15,000 km) each way—a round trip of 18,600 miles (30,000 km) in a year.

How do animals find their way during a migration? One example is salmon, which hatch out in inland streams. As young fish, they swim downriver and spend their lives in the oceans. Later, they swim all the way back to the stream where they hatched to lay their own eggs. They find the way using their very keen sense of smell, which can detect the "scent-print" of the stream where they were born.

3-second sum-up

Many animals make long journeys across the oceans.

Champion migrator

The Arctic tern wins the trophy for traveling the longest distance of any migrating animal. It travels 18,600 miles (30,000 km) a year, which adds up to 1.3 million miles (2.13 million km) over its 30-year lifespan. It flies from Greenland and the Arctic to Antarctica, which is from one end of the world to the other!

Animals such as seabirds, fish, and whales make long migrations across the oceans.

This globe shows the migration routes for the salmon, blue whale, and tern.

Pacific salmon

The salmon hatches and grows in streams but ...

... as an adult, it swims out to sea and lives in the open ocean.

Arctic tern

The tern breeds in the Arctic but ...

... flies south to feed in the Antarctic during the southern summer.

Blue whale

The blue whale gives birth in warm tropical waters but ...

... migrates to the polar regions to feed.

Ocean perils

In calm weather, the ocean looks peaceful. But all is not what it seems —dangerous reefs and shoals may lurk below the surface. Storms, hurricanes, and earthquakes can trigger giant waves that have sent many a ship to a watery grave. Even on land, you're not entirely safe—storms and tidal waves can wreck coastal towns and cities.

Ocean perils
Glossary

atmosphere The mixture of gases that surround Earth.

carbon dioxide (CO_2) A gas breathed out by people and animals and also produced by burning carbon.

current The movement of water in the ocean or a river.

eye of the storm A calm area in the center of a storm.

greenhouse effect The gradual rise in Earth's temperature, caused by naturally occurring gases, such as carbon dioxide (CO_2), which trap the heat of the sun.

polar region Area on or near the North Pole or South Pole.

pollution The addition of dirty or harmful substances to land, air, or water.

sandbank A raised area of sand below the ocean surface, which you can only see when the water level is low.

sea wall A structure built to protect a shoreline from flooding and erosion.

storm cloud A large, dark cloud that brings rain or comes before a storm.

storm surge An unusual rise in the level of the ocean near the coast, caused by wind from a severe storm.

tropical The area just above and below the equator. The climate is warm or hot, and moist all year round.

whirlpool Water moving quickly in a circular motion, produced by the meeting of opposing currents and often causing a downward spiraling action.

Hurricanes and storms

...in 30 seconds

Storms are a great danger to people either on or near the ocean. Gale-force winds whip up rough seas with waves towering over 50 ft (15 m) high. Over the centuries, storms have claimed the lives of thousands of sailors. Most dangerous of all are hurricanes, typhoons, and cylcones, which are vast, spinning storms that measure hundreds of miles across—so huge they can be seen from space.

Hurricanes begin out at sea in warm, tropical oceans. Winds blowing from opposite directions meet and start to spiral upward. Warm, moist air rises and forms huge storm clouds that shed rain, releasing heat energy. More air is sucked in at the bottom, fueling the storm.

Hurricanes contain winds whirling at more than 75 miles (120 km) per hour. Storm clouds shedding torrential rain spin around a calm area called the "eye," in the center of the hurricane.

Out to sea, these huge storms are terrifying, but they do the most damage when they reach land. The whirling column of air sucks up water, making the ocean bulge below it. When this wall of water, called a storm surge, hits land, it sweeps ashore to flood coastal towns, causing severe damage. The combination of flooding and storm-force winds can devastate coastal areas.

3-second sum-up

Hurricanes are huge spinning storms with whirling winds.

Hurricane Katrina

In 2005 Hurricane Katrina ravaged the city of New Orleans. Water sloshed over the high walls built to defend the city against flooding. Dirty, stinking water covered the city for months and 1,800 people died.

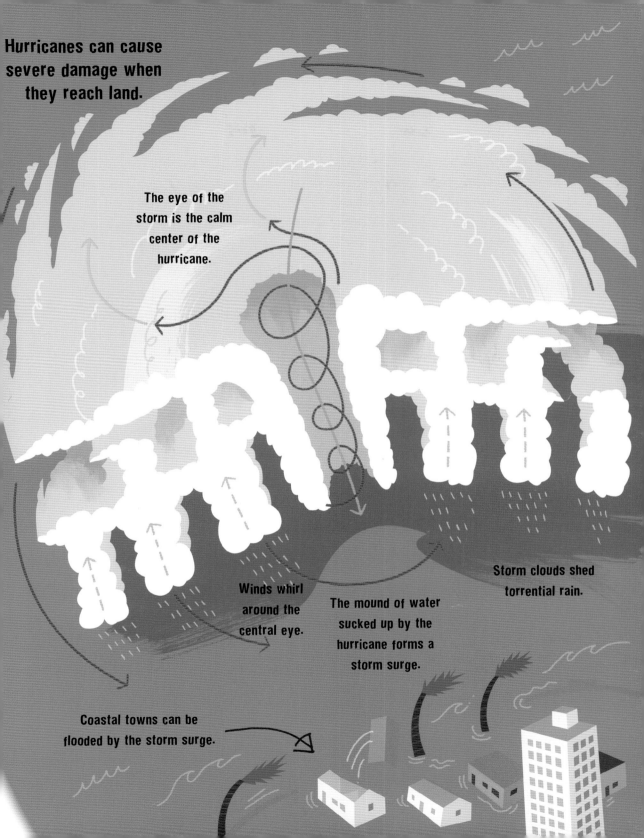

Hurricanes can cause severe damage when they reach land.

The eye of the storm is the calm center of the hurricane.

Winds whirl around the central eye.

The mound of water sucked up by the hurricane forms a storm surge.

Storm clouds shed torrential rain.

Coastal towns can be flooded by the storm surge.

Tsunamis

...in 30 seconds

When an underwater earthquake rocks the ocean floor, it causes the water above it to move violently. Waves then ripple out from this spot in all directions and race across the ocean at high speed. This is called a tsunami, or tidal wave. Tsunamis can also be caused by a violent volcanic eruption or cliff collapse that sends water sloshing everywhere.

Out to sea, tsunamis form low waves, rarely more than 18 in (0.5 m) high. Sailors hardly notice them. But when the waves reach shallow water, they rear to heights of 50 ft (15 m) or more. These huge waves then smash onto the shore with enormous force, destroying ports and towns.

On December 26th 2004, a violent earthquake struck off the coast of Sumatra, Indonesia. Just fifteen minutes later, tsunamis hit nearby coasts, flattening towns and resorts. The ripples spread right across the Indian Ocean, reaching Thailand and Malaysia 90 minutes later. After five hours, they swept ashore on the coast of Africa. More than 200,000 people died and millions of homes were destroyed.

A tsunami warning system has now been set up in the Indian Ocean. If an earthquake strikes, it triggers a warning that is sent to nearby coasts, so everyone can head inland, away from surging seas.

3-second sum-up

Tsunamis are huge waves mainly caused by earthquakes.

3-minute mission A mini-tsunami

You need: • Bowl of water • Heavy book • Table • An adult helper

1 Fill a bowl of water and put it on the table.

2 Tap under the table below the bowl with the heavy book. The ripples that spread out are like miniature tsunamis.

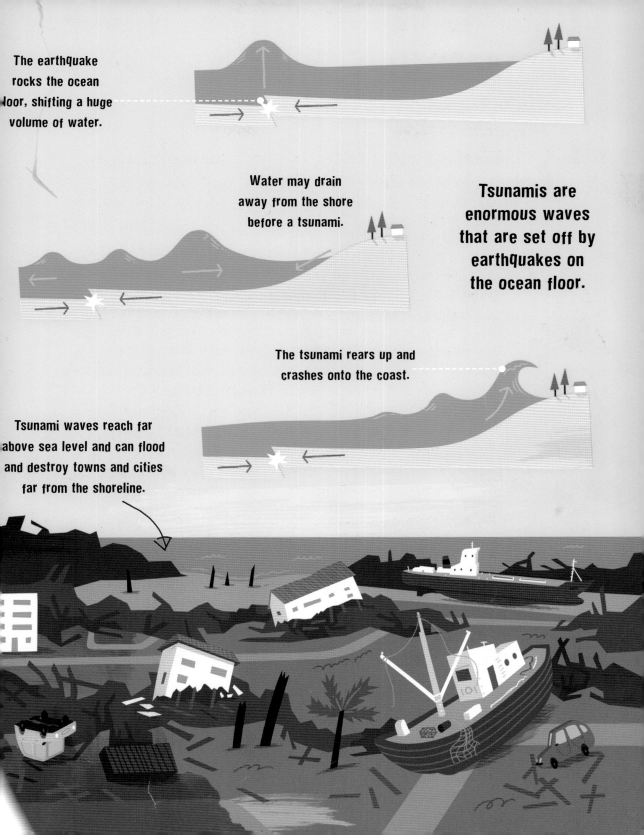

The earthquake rocks the ocean floor, shifting a huge volume of water.

Water may drain away from the shore before a tsunami.

Tsunamis are enormous waves that are set off by earthquakes on the ocean floor.

The tsunami rears up and crashes onto the coast.

Tsunami waves reach far above sea level and can flood and destroy towns and cities far from the shoreline.

Treacherous waters

...in 30 seconds

Ocean floors the world over are littered with shipwrecks—sad reminders of how dangerous oceans can be. There are many different hazards that sailors must be aware of to keep themselves safe.

Coastal features are one type of danger to look out for. In shallow waters, rocky reefs and sandbanks may lurk just beneath the surface. Unwary ships can run aground on these, and the jagged rocks can rip a hole in a ship's hull, allowing water to gush in and cause the boat to sink. Icebergs are a hazard in cold seas.

The weather can also be treacherous. Gale-force winds may drive ships onto rocks. Dense fog can hide hazards, making ships lose their bearings and run aground, or crash into one another.

Waves, tides, and currents can also spell danger for ships. Where currents collide offshore, whirlpools sometimes form. These can trap small boats and send them to their doom under the water.

Fortunately, safety measures are in place to guard against all these hazards. Lighthouses, lightships, and foghorns warn of jagged rocks. Buoys mark safe shipping lanes, helping ships to avoid collisions. Radar and satellite navigation onboard allow sailors to pinpoint their exact position and avoid hazards.

3-second sum-up

Coastal waters hold many dangers, including rocky reefs and strong currents.

Wreckers

In days gone by, people called "wreckers" used false lights to disguise the true shape of the coast and lure ships onto rocks. When the cargo washed ashore, they would steal the booty!

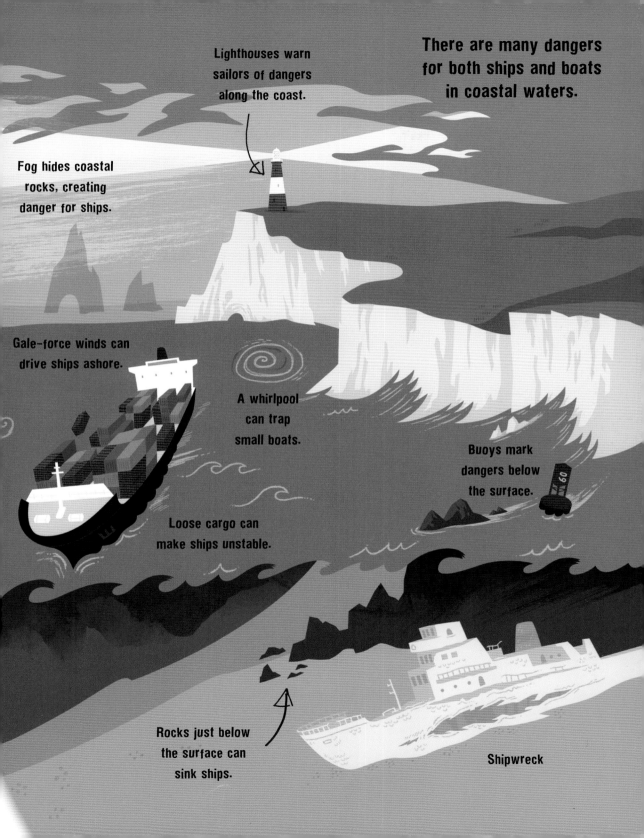

Lighthouses warn sailors of dangers along the coast.

There are many dangers for both ships and boats in coastal waters.

Fog hides coastal rocks, creating danger for ships.

Gale-force winds can drive ships ashore.

A whirlpool can trap small boats.

Buoys mark dangers below the surface.

Loose cargo can make ships unstable.

Rocks just below the surface can sink ships.

Shipwreck

Rising seas

...in 30 seconds

Earth's climate is getting warmer, which is making sea levels rise worldwide. This brings added risk of flooding to coastal towns and cities. But how and why are sea levels rising?

Changes in the atmosphere have affected the climate. High in the air, gases such as carbon dioxide (CO_2) act like the glass in a greenhouse and trap the sun's heat. Called the greenhouse effect, for millions of years it has kept the planet warm and comfortable. But now pollution from cars, factories, cities, and power plants has created more CO_2, trapping more heat and overheating the planet.

Increased temperatures are causing huge ice sheets in the polar regions to melt, releasing enormous amounts of water into the ocean. Seawater also expands as it gets warmer. All this is making sea levels rise. Towns and cities along coasts are building sea walls and other defenses to try to keep the water at bay.

3-second sum-up

Global warming is making sea levels rise, increasing the risk of coastal flooding.

3-minute mission Melting ice caps

You need: • Measuring pitcher • Clear plastic container • Ice cubes • Modeling clay • Marker

1 Mold a modeling clay "island" about 1.5 in (4 cm) high that will comfortably fit into your plastic container.

2 Lay your "island" in the container then place 3—4 ice cubes on top of the "land."

3 Add cold water to your container until the level is at least one-third of the height of your island. Use the marker to mark the water level on the outside of the container.

4 Leave your "island" for a few hours or until all the ice cubes have melted. What has happened to the water level?

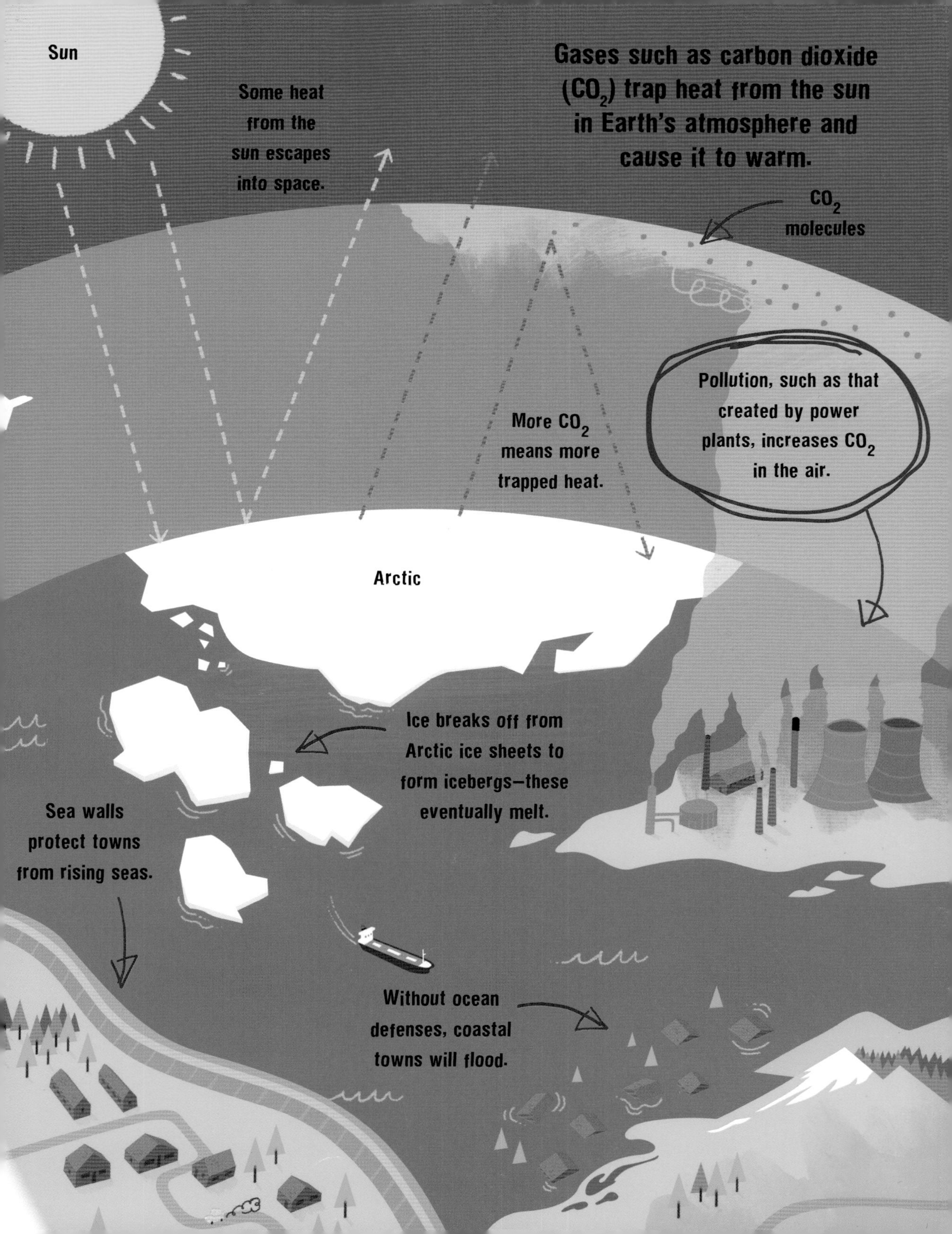

Sun

Some heat from the sun escapes into space.

Gases such as carbon dioxide (CO_2) trap heat from the sun in Earth's atmosphere and cause it to warm.

CO_2 molecules

More CO_2 means more trapped heat.

Pollution, such as that created by power plants, increases CO_2 in the air.

Arctic

Ice breaks off from Arctic ice sheets to form icebergs—these eventually melt.

Sea walls protect towns from rising seas.

Without ocean defenses, coastal towns will flood.

Exploring the oceans

Boats were invented in prehistoric times and by the late 1400s, European sailors explored the oceans. By 1900 we had accurate maps, but hardly anything was known about the dark, mysterious world below the surface. Now, thanks to modern technology, the mysteries of the deep oceans are being discovered.

Exploring the oceans
Glossary

bathyscaphe An underwater vehicle with a human operator, unlike an ROV.

clipper A fast sailing ship used in the 19th century.

container ship A ship designed to carry goods stored in containers.

dugout A simple boat made from a hollowed tree trunk.

galleon A large sailing ship used by European sailors from the 16th to 18th centuries.

geyser A hot spring that intermittently spouts jets of steam and hot water.

marine archaeologist A person who studies the remains of underwater items, such as shipwrecks, that have been left by humankind.

microscopic Something that is so small, it can only be seen using a microscope that magnifies it many times.

paddle steamer A ship powered by a steam engine that drives paddle wheels to propel the ship through the water.

prehistoric Something belonging to the time before people could write.

ROV A remotely operated underwater vehicle used for exploring the oceans.

sonar A system for finding things underwater by giving out pulses of sound.

submersible A small vehicle designed to operate underwater.

vent A crack in Earth's crust through which very hot fluids or gases rich in minerals and chemicals are released.

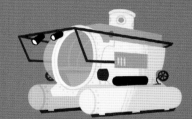

Ships and boats

...in 30 seconds

The first boats were made approximately 10,000 years ago, and were simple rafts and canoes built from materials that naturally float, such as wood and reeds. They were used for fishing and to carry people and their belongings across rivers, lakes, and coastal waters. Later, approximately 5,000 years ago, sails were first used to harness the power of the wind, making longer journeys possible. The ancient Egyptians—and later Vikings, Arabs, and the Chinese—were great boat-builders and sailors.

The 19th century was the great age of sailing. In this time, fast ships called clippers raced across the oceans with their cargoes. Steam engines—new inventions for this era—were used to power paddle wheels on the sides of ships, and later propellers at the rear. (Today, diesel engines, gas turbines, and nuclear reactors are used to drive ships' propellers.) From the mid-1800s, many ships were built of metal rather than wood.

Modern ships and boats do many jobs and come in all shapes and sizes. For example, there are enormous tankers to transport oil and gas, and large naval ships called aircraft carriers, which are used to launch planes.

3-second sum-up

Boats and ships have carried people and cargo since prehistoric times.

3-minute mission Why heavy things float

You need: • Modeling clay • Bowl of water

Many ships are now made of heavy metal, which sinks naturally. Ships float because the boat's weight is still less than the weight of water it pushes away. Shape also helps. A ship's hull is filled with air. Experiment with buoyancy using a lump of modeling clay. If you roll the clay into a ball, it will sink when placed in water. If you mold it into a boat shape with thin sides, it should float.

Today—Container ship

These ships are built to transport large
loads of cargo across the seas and oceans.

Today—Cruise ship

Passenger ships include ferries, luxury
cruise ships, and hydrofoils that skim
over the water on skis.

19th century—Clipper

In the 19th century, clippers were used
to sail across the world. They had three
masts and were very fast.

19th century—Paddle steamer

These ships were driven through
water by paddle wheels powered by
a steam engine.

**Over time, boats have developed from
small, wooden rowing boats to large
metal ships powered by diesel engines.**

5,000 years ago—Viking ship

Known as longships, Viking
ships had sails and oars.

10,000 years ago—Dugout

One of the earliest types of boat, a
dugout was a simple canoe hollowed out
of a tree trunk.

Age of discovery
...in 30 seconds

In ancient times, people like the Polynesians, Arabs, and Vikings explored the oceans, looking for new places to settle, riches such as gold and silver, or just adventure. The Polynesians explored the Pacific, Vikings crossed the Atlantic to North America, and Arabs sailed the Indian Ocean. They did all this without any maps or navigation equipment.

The age of European exploration began in the late 1400s. In 1492, Christopher Columbus crossed the Atlantic to reach the Americas. Portuguese sailor Vasco da Gama sailed the Indian Ocean in 1498 and Portuguese captain Ferdinand Magellan crossed the Pacific and sailed around the world 21 years later. The Arctic seas were explored by English captain Henry Hudson in the 1600s and James Cook explored the Southern Ocean in the 1770s.

Conditions on-board ship were tough, and food and fresh water were often scarce. The main food was rock-hard biscuits, often infested with maggots! Many sailors suffered from scurvy, a disease caused by lack of fresh fruit containing vitamin C. Discipline on ship was also harsh. If you got into trouble, you could be hit with a knotted rope.

3-second sum-up

European sailors began exploring the oceans in the late 1400s.

3-minute mission Ship mates!

Do some fun research and match the explorers (left) with their most famous ships (right). Try challenging a friend to see who can finish it first!

Christopher Columbus	the *Endeavour*
Vasco da Gama	the *Santa Maria*
Ferdinand Magellan	the *Trinidad*
Henry Hudson	the *Discovery*
James Cook	the *São Gabriel*

In the 15th and 16th centuries, explorers took to the sea, enduring hardship and danger in search of new lands.

The British explorer Captain James Cook made three long ocean voyages.

His first took him from the UK across the Atlantic to the Pacific and Australia, before returning to the UK.

Drinking water was scarce so sailors drank beer and rum instead.

Potatoes were brought to Europe.

Food was often infested with maggots.

Punishments included keel hauling, which meant a person was tied to a rope and pulled under the ship.

Exploring underwater

...in 30 seconds

The Ancient Greeks experimented with the diving bell—a bell-shaped barrel filled with air and open at the bottom—as early as the 4th century BCE. But underwater exploration as we know it did not begin until the 1800s, when diving suits—rubberized suits with heavy helmets—were invented. However, divers breathed air pumped from the surface through a tube, and so had limited mobility.

In the 1940s, the invention of the aqualung for scuba diving revolutionized underwater exploration. With a tank of compressed air strapped on, a diver could now roam freely. Scuba divers can reach depths of up to 160 ft (50 m), but those descending deeper than this need to use a different mix of compressed gases to reduce the risk of the "bends"—a potentially deadly condition where bubbles of nitrogen gas form in the diver's blood. All divers must ascend slowly to avoid the bends.

While scuba divers explore the surface waters, scientists dive to the deep oceans in small submarines called submersibles. Remotely Operated Vehicles, or ROVs, are craft without a crew that scan, measure, and take samples from the ocean depths. In 1960, two brave explorers reached the ocean's deepest point, Challenger Deep in the Mariana Trench—36,000 ft (10,920 m) below the surface, in a craft called a bathyscaphe.

3-second sum-up

Divers, submarines, and submersibles explore underwater.

Sonar

A system called sonar is used to map the ocean floor. A ship or underwater scanner aims pulses of sound at the ocean floor and measures the time taken by the echoes to bounce off the bottom. Sonar is used to locate underwater ridges, trenches, and hills called seamounts.

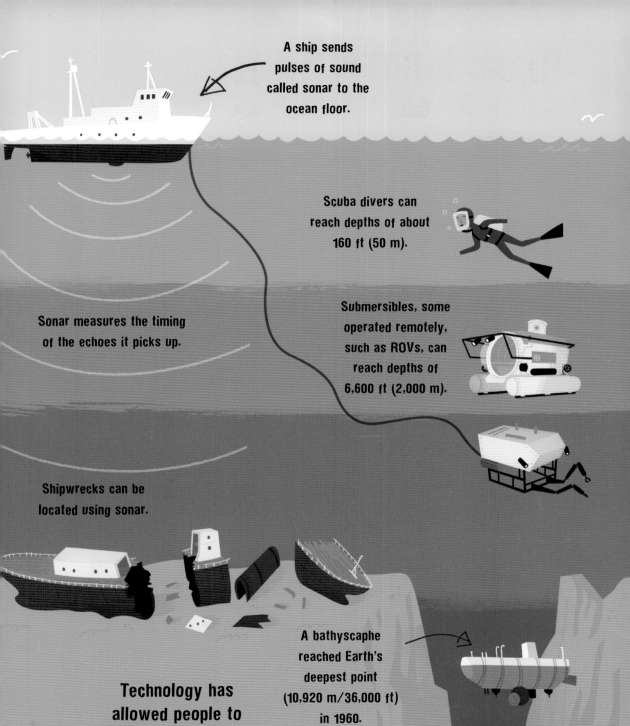

A ship sends pulses of sound called sonar to the ocean floor.

Scuba divers can reach depths of about 160 ft (50 m).

Sonar measures the timing of the echoes it picks up.

Submersibles, some operated remotely, such as ROVs, can reach depths of 6,600 ft (2,000 m).

Shipwrecks can be located using sonar.

A bathyscaphe reached Earth's deepest point (10,920 m/36,000 ft) in 1960.

Technology has allowed people to explore deeper and deeper parts of the oceans.

Black smokers

...in 30 seconds

In 1977 scientists exploring an underwater ridge in the Pacific made an amazing discovery. They found tall, rocky chimneys belching dark clouds of hot water and minerals. These weird formations, called black smokers, have now been found in other parts of the deep oceans.

Black smokers form at vents or cracks in the rocks of volcanic ridges. Seawater seeping into the cracks is heated by molten rock below and mixes with minerals. When it is scalding hot, it shoots out of the vent like a geyser. Over time, the minerals deposited around the vents build up to form chimneys up to 33 ft (10 m) high.

Black smokers are extraordinary formations and amazingly they are home to living things found nowhere else on Earth. Strange tubeworms up to 10 ft (3 m) long thrive by the vents, along with snails, eyeless shrimps, spider crabs, and fish called eelpouts.

These creatures endure poisonous minerals and water heated to above 570°F (300°C). Some survive thanks to the presence of microscopic bacteria on and around them, which use the minerals to make food.

3-second sum-up

Black smokers are volcanic vents that gush hot, dark water.

3-minute mission Make a black smoker

You need: • Small plastic bottle • Vinegar • Plastic dish tub •Food coloring • Baking soda

1 Fill the plastic bottle half-full of vinegar. Stand it in the dish tub.

2 Add a few drops of two different colors of food coloring to make the vinegar as dark as possible.

3 Now add 1 tablespoon of baking soda. Stand back and watch your black smoker erupt!

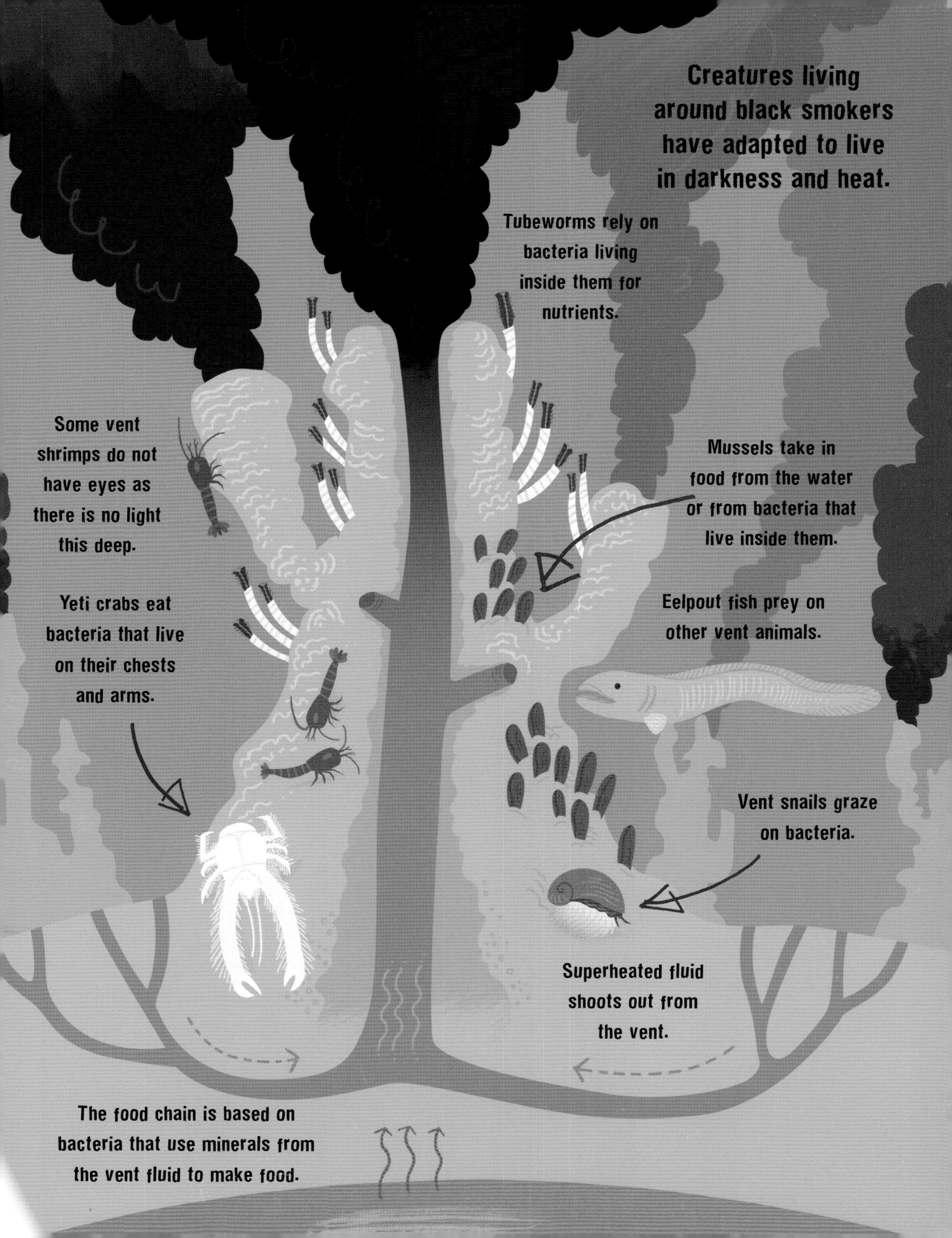

Creatures living
around black smokers
have adapted to live
in darkness and heat.

Tubeworms rely on
bacteria living
inside them for
nutrients.

Some vent
shrimps do not
have eyes as
there is no light
this deep.

Mussels take in
food from the water
or from bacteria that
live inside them.

Yeti crabs eat
bacteria that live
on their chests
and arms.

Eelpout fish prey on
other vent animals.

Vent snails graze
on bacteria.

Superheated fluid
shoots out from
the vent.

The food chain is based on
bacteria that use minerals from
the vent fluid to make food.

Diving for treasure

...in 30 seconds

In some parts of the oceans, fabulous treasure such as gold, silver, and pearls can be found on the ocean floor. Most of this has come from old shipwrecks, but coastal cities sunk by earthquakes or tsunamis may also contain precious items. Marine archaeologists and salvage experts find sunken treasure and bring it to the surface.

In the past, anyone could dive for sunken treasure, but now marine archaeology is controlled by law and carried out using state-of-the-art technology. Wrecks and sunken cities can be located using sonar. In shallow water, marine archaeologists can dive down to take photographs. Blowing or sucking machines are used to clear sand, mud, and debris away from wrecks.

Submersibles and ROVs are used to locate wrecks sunk in deeper water. In 1985 scientists located the wreck of the ocean liner *Titanic* on the bed of the Atlantic Ocean, more than 12,000 ft (3,700 m) below the surface. After 70 years on the bottom, treasures from the famous ship, sunk by an iceberg, were rescued from the depths.

One of the richest treasure ships was located in the Caribbean in 1977. A Spanish galleon, the *Tolosa*, had been sunk by a hurricane in 1724. The wreck contained silver, gold, pearls, and diamond jewelry.

3-second sum-up

Marine archaeologists locate wrecks and sunken cities and bring treasure to the surface.

Lost city

In the 100s BCE Queen Cleopatra of Egypt built a palace at Alexandria on the shores of the Mediterranean. Later, earthquakes and tidal waves drowned the city. In 1996 archaeologists located the palace. Statues and other priceless treasures were recovered from the site.

Deep-sea divers and archaeologists work under the ocean to find shipwrecks and treasure.

Archaeologists record finds underwater before bringing them to the surface.

Gold coins

The *Tolosa* shipwreck contained gold, silver, and diamonds.

Divers move a grid called a quadrant along the ocean floor to help them find small items.

Using the oceans

The oceans contain vital resources, providing food, minerals, and energy. For thousands of years, we have used the seas for trade and transport. All over the world, cities, ports, and resorts have grown up by the coast. However, our use of the oceans is now causing problems such as pollution.

Using the oceans
Glossary

conservation Protecting things found in nature such as wildlife, and keeping the environment clean and healthy.

detergent A substance used for cleaning.

fertilizer A chemical or natural substance added to soil to help crops and plants grow.

food chain A system where small animals are eaten by larger animals, which, in turn, are food for even larger animals.

Industrial Revolution A period of time, in the 18th to 19th centuries, when things began to be made by machines in factories, requiring more fuel and energy.

marine habitat The natural environment of something living in the ocean.

marine reserve An area of the ocean that has legal protection against fishing or development.

mineral A substance, naturally present on Earth, and not formed from animal or vegetable matter; for example, gold.

oil slick A layer of oil, which usually comes from damaged oil containers at sea, that floats on water and can damage animals and plants.

pesticide A substance used for killing insects or other organisms harmful to crops or animals.

pollute To add dirty or harmful substances to land, air, or water.

sewage Used water, such as water from your washing machine, kitchen sink, bathtub, and toilet.

sustainable To use things, such as the ocean's natural resources, in a way that means they will still be there in the future and not used up.

toxic waste Waste material that can harm living creatures.

Food from the sea

...in 30 seconds

Since ancient times, the animals and plants found in and around the seas and oceans have provided food for people. Everything from fish, shrimps, crabs, and lobsters to seaweed can be eaten.

On the coast, people fish using traditional hooks and small nets, but commercial fishing is now a high-tech business. Modern fishing fleets have sonar to locate fish shoals and use huge nets to capture them. Small fishing boats must return to harbor daily, but factory ships freeze their catch on board so that they can stay at sea for days and catch even more fish.

Every year, a staggering 90 million tons of fish are taken from the world's seas and oceans. Many species of fish have become scarce. Fish numbers drop steeply when there are not enough adult fish left to breed. This problem is called overfishing. In some waters, fish such as cod have almost completely died out. Creatures such as dolphins, seals, and turtles also die in fishing nets.

So what can we do to protect fish stocks? Fishing nations set limits on the number of fish that can be caught. Fish farming can also help—for example, mussels are reared in baskets on the coast, to ease the pressure on fish in the wild. We can also eat species of fish that are less scarce.

3-second sum-up

Fish are a vital source of food, but overfishing has made some species rare.

Seaweed scavenger hunt!

Not only can you eat seaweed—many household products contain it as well. Go through your home and look at the ingredients in items such as cosmetics, cleaning products, or basic pantry items such as food coloring. If a product contains "alginates," "carrageenan," or "beta-carotene," you are looking at something that contains seaweed!

The oceans provide a wide variety of food, from fish and shellfish to seaweed.

Fish is transported in refrigerated trucks to keep it fresh.

Herring

Crab

Shrimp

Mussels

Lobster

Oyster

Clams

Salmon

Mackerel

Riches from the oceans

...in 30 seconds

The oceans hold many natural treasures besides food.
Minerals such as zinc, tin, copper, and nickel can be found in rocks on the ocean floor, as can gold and diamonds, carried out to sea by rivers. The deep oceans also hold valuable lumps of rock called manganese nodules, which contain minerals, but bringing these minerals to the surface can be difficult and expensive.

As well as minerals, the oceans hold valuable fuels such as oil and natural gas. When scientists discover pockets of oil and gas in rocks on the ocean floor, an oil platform can be built to extract them. The oil rig drills down under the ocean floor to reach the fuel and then pumps it up to the surface to be taken where it is needed.

Oil and gas are not the only source of energy in the oceans—tidal stations harness the movement energy of the tide to make electricity. While oil and gas will eventually run out, tidal energy is limitless, so is more sustainable.

3-second sum-up

The oceans provide useful minerals, fuels, and energy.

3-minute mission Make salt

Much of the salt that flavors our food comes from the ocean. Seawater is channeled into shallow basins on the coast. The water evaporates in the sun, leaving the salt to be collected. You can try this at home.

You need: • Shallow bowl • Salt • Sun

1 Fill a shallow bowl with water.

2 Add three tablespoons of salt and stir until all the salt is dissolved.

3 Leave the bowl in a sunny place. Check it every day.

4 Eventually all the water will evaporate, leaving a salty crust.

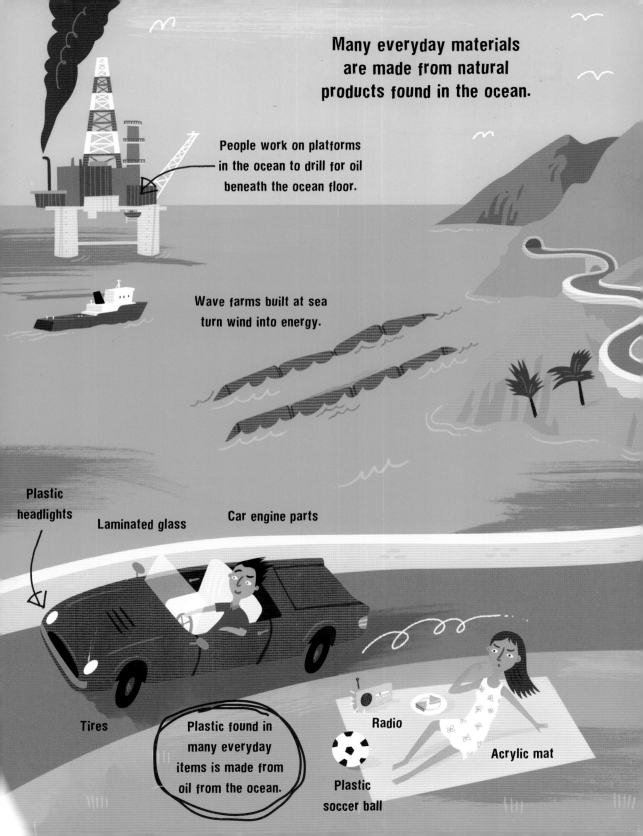

Many everyday materials are made from natural products found in the ocean.

People work on platforms in the ocean to drill for oil beneath the ocean floor.

Wave farms built at sea turn wind into energy.

Plastic headlights

Laminated glass

Car engine parts

Tires

Plastic found in many everyday items is made from oil from the ocean.

Radio

Plastic soccer ball

Acrylic mat

Living by the sea

...in 30 seconds

Coastal areas were among the first places where people settled. As well as food, the ocean provided a means of transportation, and often defense against invaders. Coasts are still popular places to live, work, or just relax on vacation.

In ancient times, villages developed on bays and natural harbors that could shelter boats. People also settled along rivers leading to the ocean, which could be used to move people and goods inland. As new lands across the oceans were discovered and trade expanded, small coastal villages grew into busy ports with sprawling docks.

After the Industrial Revolution began in the 1700s, factories were built to process goods that arrived by sea, and ports became centers of manufacturing. Now many of the world's largest cities are on coasts.

People began to visit the seaside on vacation over 200 years ago. The late 1950s saw the start of cheap air travel, which allowed people to take vacations abroad. Resorts sprang up on remote beaches all over the world. Now millions flock to the seaside to swim, dive, surf, sail, and snorkel—or just enjoy the sunshine.

3-second sum-up

People living by the sea can use it for work, trade, food, and pleasure.

City on the sea

Venice, Italy, is a unique city that is actually built on the water on 118 small islands. There are no roads or cars so people use boats to get around. Venice developed hundreds of years ago as an important city because merchants could come from all around the world by ship to trade goods. Today, however, Venice is sinking. This is partly because sea levels are rising.

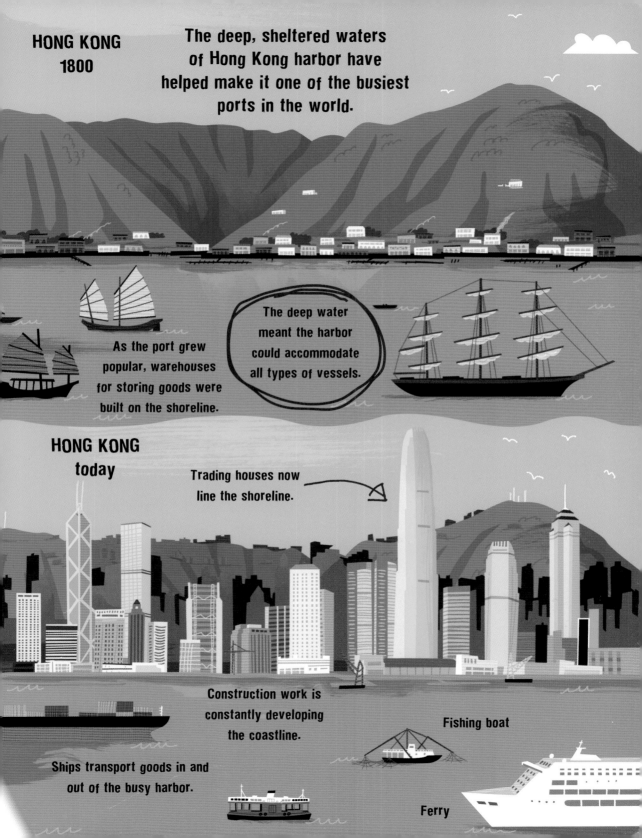

HONG KONG 1800

The deep, sheltered waters of Hong Kong harbor have helped make it one of the busiest ports in the world.

As the port grew popular, warehouses for storing goods were built on the shoreline.

The deep water meant the harbor could accommodate all types of vessels.

HONG KONG today

Trading houses now line the shoreline.

Construction work is constantly developing the coastline.

Fishing boat

Ships transport goods in and out of the busy harbor.

Ferry

Ocean pollution

...in 30 seconds

As the world population has grown, so has our use of the oceans. Unfortunately many of our activities cause pollution, which is harmful to marine life and habitats.

Waste and poisonous chemicals are dumped in the water or burned at sea, which causes air pollution. Waste from the land also enters the ocean through rivers. Cities, factories, and mines on coasts and rivers produce sewage, detergents, and other types of dangerous waste. Fertilizers and pesticides used on farms drain away into rivers, which empty into the ocean.

For centuries people thought the oceans were so huge this wouldn't matter. We now know dangerous waste in the water is absorbed by small sea creatures and carried up the food chain. Poisons, such as mercury, build up in predators such as dolphins and fish such as tuna. People in turn eat the tuna. Waste also harms coral reefs, which need pure water to thrive.

Oil spills are another source of pollution. These happen when tankers run aground or when oil wells spring a leak. In 2010 an explosion on an oil rig in the Gulf of Mexico created a huge oil slick that spread over 2,500 sq miles (6,500 sq km) of ocean. It took several years and billions of dollars to clear it up.

3-second sum-up

Waste, litter, and oil spills pollute the oceans.

Litter

The litter that we drop can end up in the ocean, where it may wash ashore on beaches. Plastic, glass, metal, and old fishing nets end up on remote islands, where they can choke or trap young birds, seals, and turtles. Out in the open ocean, there are floating "islands" of plastic litter that drift with currents and tides.

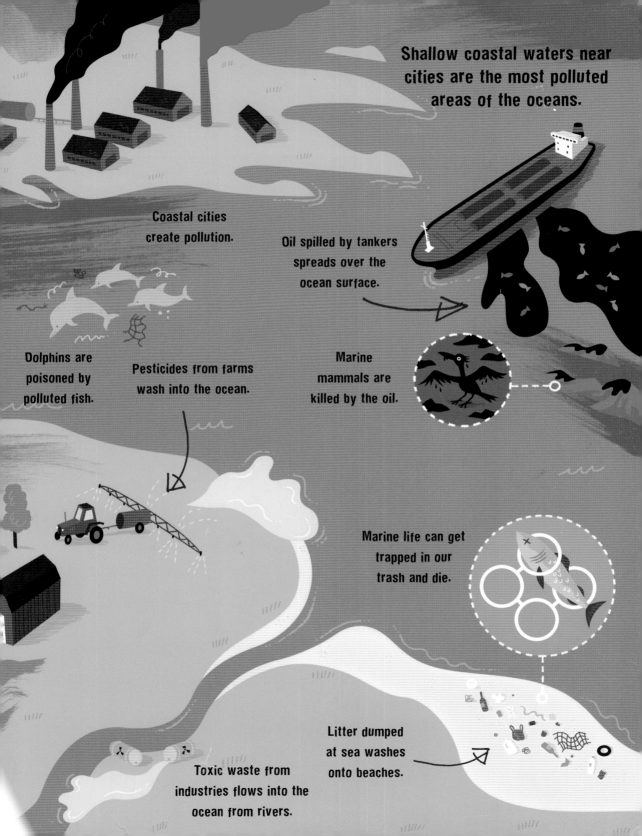

Shallow coastal waters near cities are the most polluted areas of the oceans.

Coastal cities create pollution.

Oil spilled by tankers spreads over the ocean surface.

Dolphins are poisoned by polluted fish.

Pesticides from farms wash into the ocean.

Marine mammals are killed by the oil.

Marine life can get trapped in our trash and die.

Toxic waste from industries flows into the ocean from rivers.

Litter dumped at sea washes onto beaches.

Protecting the oceans
...in 30 seconds

The oceans are in trouble, with threats from pollution, overfishing, and climate change. But there are things we can do to help. More and more people are getting involved in conservation work to protect the oceans and preserve them for the future. The oceans affect the whole planet, so anything we can do to help them will make the planet a cleaner, healthier place.

Governments help with conservation by setting limits to prevent overfishing, banning the dumping of waste into the oceans, and setting up marine reserves where no fishing can take place. Most governments have also made practices such as whaling illegal, which has allowed the numbers of whales to begin recovering. All of these changes can have a positive impact on the oceans and the world.

But conservation can be done on a small scale as well—we can all help to make a big difference by helping in our local areas and joining in the global effort to save our seas.

3-second sum-up

Marine conservation is work done to protect the oceans.

3-minute mission Save our seas!

We can all help to protect the oceans. Here are some ideas:

- Join with some friends to raise money for an eco-project—maybe there's a local marine or river habitat that needs help.

- Reduce the effects of climate change by using less energy. Write reminder notes to encourage your family to turn off lights and computers when they're not using them.

- Reuse as many items at home as possible. Plastic bottles, cardboard, and scrap paper are great for craft activities.

- Get together with friends to organize a beach or river cleanup. Wear gloves and ask an adult to supervise.

Governments, conservation organizations, and ordinary people can all help to protect the oceans.

Bans on whaling protect rare species.

Marine reserves protect habitats such as coral reefs.

Beach cleanups remove litter that can harm animals.

Discover more

NON-FICTION BOOKS

Alien Deep by Bradley Hague
National Geographic Kids, 2012

DK Eyewitness Guide: Ocean by Miranda Macquitty
Dorling Kindersley, 1995

DK Eyewitness Guide: Seashore by Steve Parker
Dorling Kindersley, 1998

DK Eyewitness Explorers: Seashore by David Burnie
Dorling Kindersley, 1997

DK Guide to the Oceans by Frances Dipper
Dorling Kindersley, 2002

Geographywise: Coasts by Jen Green
Wayland, 2010

The Oceans Atlas by Anita Ganeri
Dorling Kindersley, 1994

The World's Oceans by Jen Green
Franklin Watts, 2009

Weird Sea Creatures by Laura Marsh
National Geographic Readers, 2012

DVDs—suitable for all ages

Blue Planet: Complete BBC Series Narrated by David Attenborough
BBC, 2005

Blue Planet 3D Aquarium
Focus Multimedia Ltd, 2008

Ocean Life: From A to Z by Annie Crawley
Reader's Digest, 2007

WEBSITES

Information and facts about oceans

Save the Seas
http://www.savethesea.org/STS%20ocean_facts.htm

Sea and Sky
http://www.seasky.org/

US National Oceanic and Atmospheric Administration (NOAA)
http://www.noaa.gov/ocean.html

Ocean life
BBC Nature: Wildlife of the Deep Ocean
http://www.bbc.co.uk/nature/habitats/Deep_sea

National Geographic
http://ocean.nationalgeographic.com/ocean/ocean-life/

National Geographic: Deep Sea
http://ocean.nationalgeographic.com/ocean/
photos/deep-sea-creatures/

Ocean conservation

The MarineBio Conservation Society
http://marinebio.org/oceans/creatures.asp

The Ocean Foundation
http://www.oceanfdn.org/
newsroom/about-our-oceans

Worldwide Fund for Nature (WWF)
http://www.worldwildlife.org/habitats/oceans

Index

Index